DECK THE HALLS
WITH BUDDY HOLLY

And Other Misheard Christmas Lyrics

GAVIN EDWARDS
ILLUSTRATED BY TED STEARN

HarperPerennial

A Division of HarperCollinsPublishers

FIRST EDITION

Designed by Laura Lindgren

Library of Congress Cataloging-in-Publication Data
Edwards, Gavin, 1968–
    Deck the halls with Buddy Holly : and other misheard Christmas lyrics / Gavin Edwards.
        p.   cm.
    Includes index.
    ISBN 0–06–095293–8
    1. Popular music—Texts—Humor. 2. Christmas music—Texts—Humor.
I. Title.
ML65.E29 1998
782342164'0268—dc21   98-23757

98 99 00 01 02 RRD   10 9 8 7 6 5 4 3 2 1

For Jilly, who makes my days
merry and bright

Introduction

Every year at Christmastime, your radio sounds like it's been taken over by rogue bands of Santa's elves. Stations set aside their regular programming for a steady diet of fa-la-la-la-la and rum-pa-pum-pum, which ends abruptly on December 26. It's not too hard to imagine the heavily armed elves brandishing machine guns at the kneecaps of innocent DJs.

No other holiday heralds its arrival this way. April does not come with a blitzkrieg of songs about the Easter Bunny. Love songs play all year round, not just in the vicinity of Valentine's Day. Every Thanksgiving, we can note the steady absence of top-forty artists releasing albums filled with songs about turkeys. (Admittedly, there are CDs in the stores that *are* turkeys, but that's something altogether different.)

Of course, with so many songs filled with Christmas cheer flooding the airwaves in December (and yes, it's a painful experience if the onslaught begins earlier than that), it's not surprising that some listeners become, well, a little confused. They hear Bruce Springsteen singing "Santa Claus is Comin' to Town" and think that it's actually "Santa Claus is Comin' to Tan." Or maybe they transform "round yon virgin" in "Silent Night" into a fat guy sitting in the manger: Round John Virgin. Although these hapless listeners don't realize it, they've stumbled onto a Christmas mondegreen—and that's where I come into the equation.

You see, I collect mondegreens. The word *mondegreen* is the technical term for a misheard lyric—Sylvia Wright coined it in a 1954 *Atlantic* article. If your dictionary's big enough, you'll find it listed and defined there. But if what you crave is not a definition but the authentic mondegreens of our times, I suggest you consult my previous three books: *'Scuse Me While I Kiss This Guy and Other Misheard Lyrics*, *He's Got the Whole World in His Pants and More Misheard Lyrics*, and *When a Man Loves a Walnut and Even More Misheard Lyrics*.

The contents of this book come from two primary sources: radio Christmas hits misinterpreted by listeners and Yuletide favorites mangled by carolers. Since so many Christmas tunes are standards, most of the songs in *Deck the Halls with Buddy Holly and Other Misheard Christmas Lyrics* are listed by title only, without any particular musician's name attached. (The exceptions come when a song has been done exclusively by one artist, like Prince's "Another Lonely Christmas" or the Smashing Pumpkins' "Christmastime," or when an artist has added an original lyric to a standard, like Peggy Lee with "Santa Claus Is Comin' to Town.") Hanson notwithstanding, not as many acts release full Christmas albums as was once the case: There are more one-off singles and tracks donated to charity compilations, like the Very Special Christmas series. But all these songs have a life of their own, sung by professionals as well as people like you and me.

Many Christmas songs get recorded over and over: "Silent Night," to pick one example, has been done over the years by artists including Elvis Presley, Stevie Nicks, and John Denver and the Muppets. You might think that "Santa Baby" is the exclusive property of Eartha Kitt, but there are lots of people who only know Madonna's take on the song. So the upshot is that not every version of every song will reflect every mondegreen in this book. To cite just one example, when Chris Cornell of Soundgarden recorded "Ave Maria," he managed to make the title sound like "Ow, Marie, yuck!" I don't think anybody else has pulled off this particular vocal trick. (Furthermore, Cornell's rendition of the line "Oh, listen to a maiden's prayer" landed somewhere closer to "Oh, listen to the lady of spades.") But you'll be amazed at how many songs produce repeated confusion across multiple versions.

Part of the reason is that Christmas music is passed down from generation to generation. Although there are periodic new additions to the canon—just think of "Grandma Got Run Over by a Reindeer"—many of our favorites date back decades or even centuries. As a result, they are littered with words and phrases not in our 1990s vocabulary, like "in excelsis Deo" and "figgy pudding."

Overcome by too much Christmas cheer, or maybe just an excess of eggnog, some people interpret perfectly ordinary, non-seasonal pop music as having hidden Christmas meanings. For example, to some ears Billy Idol's "Dancing with Myself" is actually an ode to a disco at the North Pole: "Dancing with Nice Elves." I've collected a sampling of these lyrics in an appendix, titled "It's Beginning to Sound a Lot Like Christmas."

A final note: I am saddened to report that Hanukkah, Kwanzaa, and New Year's Eve do not have musical traditions comparable to that of Christmas. There've been some heavy hitters working on Christmas music: everyone from Handel to Run-D.M.C. New Year's Eve really has only "Auld Lang Syne"; nevertheless, people *still* manage to mangle the lyrics, rendering "Should old acquaintance be forgot" as "Should all equations be for God?" And until Adam Sandler came along, the best Hanukkah had to offer was "dreidel dreidel dreidel, I made you out of clay." But at least one person thought that Elton John recorded a song in celebration of the Festival of Lights. An easy mistake, if you're convinced that the chorus of "Philadelphia Freedom" is actually "Phil, I got me a dreidel." So have the merriest of Christmases—and this year, if you go out caroling and don't know the words, try to sing louder than everybody else.

Here's how most of the mondegreens in *Deck the Halls with Buddy Holly* are printed:

Wrong lyric

Song title

Right lyric

When a particular artist is credited, we print the information like this:

Wrong lyric

Song title, ARTIST

Right lyric

And finally, when there are multiple mishearings of the same line, we set them apart in this fashion:

❋ First wrong lyric

❋ Second wrong lyric

Song title

Right lyric

Olive, the other reindeer

"Rudolph the Red-Nosed Reindeer"

All of the other reindeer

✳ Deck the halls with buns of Holland

✳ Deck the halls with bows of folly

✳ Deck the halls with Buddy Holly

"Deck the Halls"

Deck the halls with boughs of holly

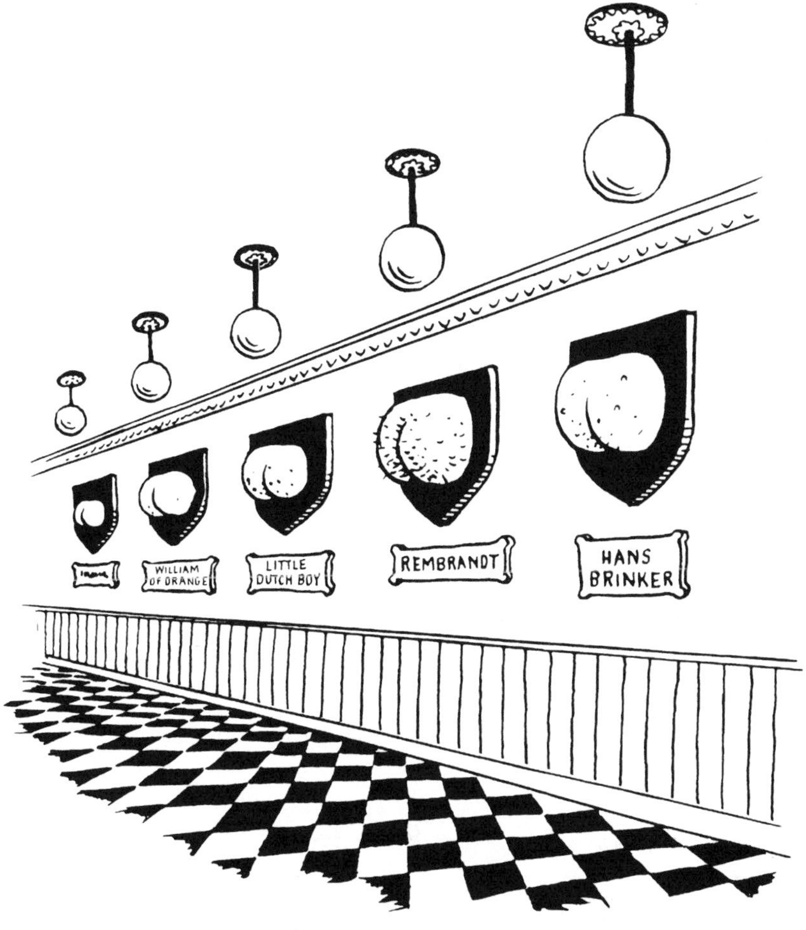
WILLIAM OF ORANGE
LITTLE DUTCH BOY
REMBRANDT
HANS BRINKER

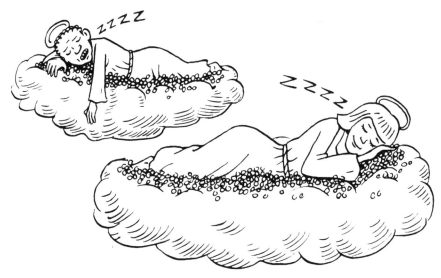

Sleep in heavenly peas

"*Silent Night*"

Sleep in heavenly peace

You'll tell Carol, "Be a skunk, I require"

"The Christmas Song"

Yuletide carols sung by a choir

You're a vowel, Mr. Grinch

"You're a Mean One, Mr. Grinch"

You're a vile one, Mr. Grinch

We three kings of porridge and tar

"We Three Kings"

We three kings of Orient are

In the fly place is the Yule log

"Christmas in Hollis," RUN-D.M.C.

In the fireplace is the Yule log

On the first day of Christmas,
my tulip gave to me

"The Twelve Days of Christmas"

*On the first day of Christmas,
my true love gave to me*

In the meadow we can build a snowman,
then pretend that he is sparse and brown

"Winter Wonderland"

---

*In the meadow we can build a snowman,
then pretend that he is Parson Brown*

An eggshell stable

"Angels We Have Heard on High"

In excelsis Deo

Radiate meat from your holy place

"Silent Night"

Radiant beams from thy holy face

Now the goo is on the table

"Grandma Got Run Over By a Reindeer," ELMO & PATSY

Now the goose is on the table

He's making a list, chicken and rice

"Santa Claus Is Comin' to Town"

He's making a list, checking it twice

To the North Pole, force it in

"All I Want for Christmas Is You,"

MARIAH CAREY

To the North Pole, for St. Nick

Long-legged worm

"O Holy Night"

Long lay the world

May your days be merry in brine

"White Christmas"

May your days be merry and bright

❄ Too sporty for his feed

❄ Too portly for his feet

"Jingle Bells"

Two-forty for his speed

Ten lawyers leaving

"*The Twelve Days of Christmas*"

Ten lords a-leaping

My baby was shot yesterday

"*Santa Claus,*"

SONNY BOY WILLIAMSON

My baby went shoppin' yesterday

The greatest gift they'll get this year is flies

"Do They Know It's Christmas?"

BAND AID

The greatest gift they'll get this year is life

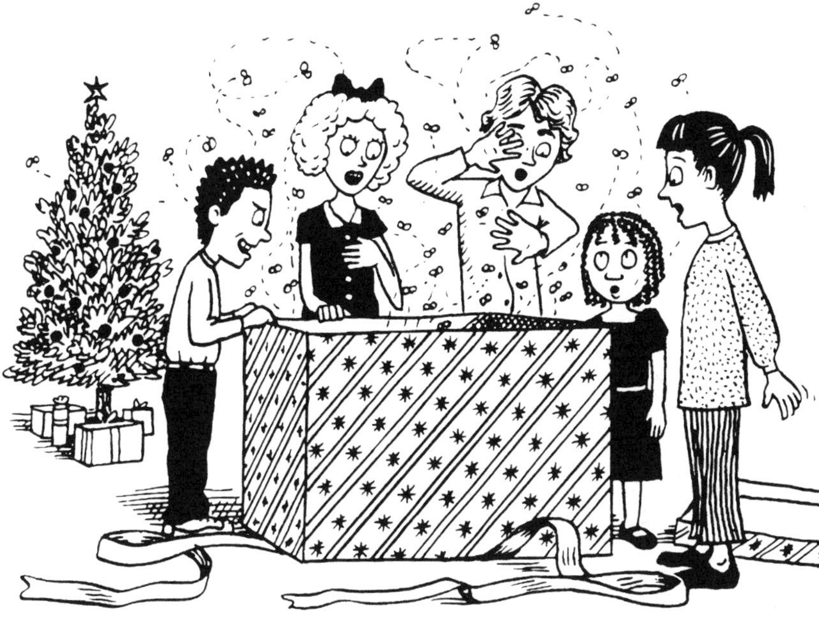

Goddamn sinners reckon so

"Hark! The Herald Angels Sing"

God and sinners reconciled

Sing on eggs all stationed

"O Come All Ye Faithful"

Sing in exultation

Christmas tongue in ear

---

*"The Chipmunk Song
(Christmas Don't Be Late),"*

THE CHIPMUNKS

Christmastime is near

Secretly against your house the fondue waits

"Christmastime,"

SMASHING PUMPKINS

Secretly against your house the fun awaits

The purple berries and fries were there

"I Saw Three Ships"

The Virgin Mary and Christ were there

Stabbing fight, hold the knife

"Silent Night"

Silent night, holy night

He will bring us windows and limes

"Do You Hear What I Hear?"

He will bring us goodness and light

Santa Claus, they're so rough, they need to sew

"Santa Claus Go Straight to the Ghetto," JAMES BROWN

Santa Claus, the soul brothers need you so

NOW THERE'S ALSO THE DOUBLE STITCH...

✳ Oh come, hoggy faithful

✳ Oh come, froggy faithful

"O Come All Ye Faithful"

O come all ye faithful

Nine lazy Hansons

"The Twelve Days of Christmas"

Nine ladies dancing

Please bring us some friggin' pudding

"We Wish You a Merry Christmas"

Please bring us some figgy pudding

The fire is soda, like full

"Let It Snow!
Let It Snow! Let It Snow!"

The fire is so delightful

What apostles aren't for free?

"Christmas," THE WHO

What parcels are for free?

❊ Chet's nuts roasting on an open fire

❊ Chipmunks roasting on an open fire

"The Christmas Song"

Chestnuts roasting on an open fire

Later on, we'll perspire, as we dream by the fire

"Winter Wonderland"

Later on, we'll conspire, as we dream by the fire

King forever, seasoned leather

"We Three Kings"

King forever, ceasing never

✳ Police have my dad

✳ For those smelling bad

✳ Police Doggy Dogg

"Feliz Navidad"

Feliz Navidad

I will behead you for Christmas

"I Will Be Hating You for Christmas," EVERCLEAR

I will be hating you for Christmas

You shouldn't trick my mice

"*Merry Christmas Baby*"

You sure do treat me nice

Don, we now are gayest parents

"*Hark! The Herald Angels Sing*"

Don we now our gay apparel

From angels binging near the Earth

"It Came Upon a Midnight Clear"

From angels bending near the Earth

Noel, Noel, Barney's the king of Israel

"The First Noel"

Noel, Noel, born is the king of Israel

Children, go warm and sandy

"Children, Go Where I Send Thee"

Children, go where I send thee

Cut off Santa Claus and his Polish reindeer

"(All I Want for Christmas Is) My Two Front Teeth," SPIKE JONES

Good old Santa Claus and all his reindeer

Ship her cake, at the site

"Silent Night"

Shepherds quake at the sight

Angels we have heard on high,
sweetly singing or complaining

"Angels We Have Heard on High"

*Angels we have heard on high,
sweetly singing o'er the plains/And*

Eat snow and made meat on some other day

"Snoopy's Christmas,"

THE ROYAL GUARDSMEN

Each knowing they'd meet on some other day

Rudolph the red-nosed reindeer,
you'll go drown in Listerine

"Rudolph the Red-Nosed Reindeer"

*Rudolph the red-nosed reindeer,
you'll go down in history*

ALL I SAID WAS,
"YOUR BREATH REALLY
STINKS!"

I don't know if there'll be snow
but have a cup of cheese

"A Holly Jolly Christmas"

I don't know if there'll be snow
but have a cup of cheer

Seven warts on women

"The Twelve Days of Christmas"

Seven swans a-swimmin'

Baby, you promised me Sizzlean

"Another Lonely Christmas,"

PRINCE

Baby, you promised me you'd never leave

53

What fun it is to write and
sing a slaying song to knives

"Jingle Bells"

What fun it is to ride and
sing a sleighing song tonight

Jeff's disabled under the tree

"Santa Baby"

Just slip a sable under the tree

With the jelly toast proclaim

"Hark! The Herald Angels Sing"

With th'angelic host proclaim

It's Christmastime, a howl and squeeze

"Christmas in Hollis,"

RUN-D.M.C.

It's Christmastime in Hollis, Queens

That's when those blue evergreens start callin'

"Blue Christmas"

That's when those blue memories start callin'

Christmas is now drawing a turkey hand

*"Christmas Is Now
Drawing Near at Hand"*

Christmas is now drawing near at hand

Get a yuck, get a yuck

"Sleigh Ride"

Giddy-up, giddy-up

Round John Virgin

"*Silent Night*"

Round yon virgin

Dick the hog

"Deck the Halls"

Deck the halls

Massage me safely to McDonald's
_____

"*Ave Maria*"
_____

We slumber safely to the morrow

Check for snipping at your nose
_____

"*The Christmas Song*"
_____

Jack Frost nipping at your nose

Hear the snow crunch, see the kids punch

"Silver Bells"

Hear the snow crunch, see the kids bunch

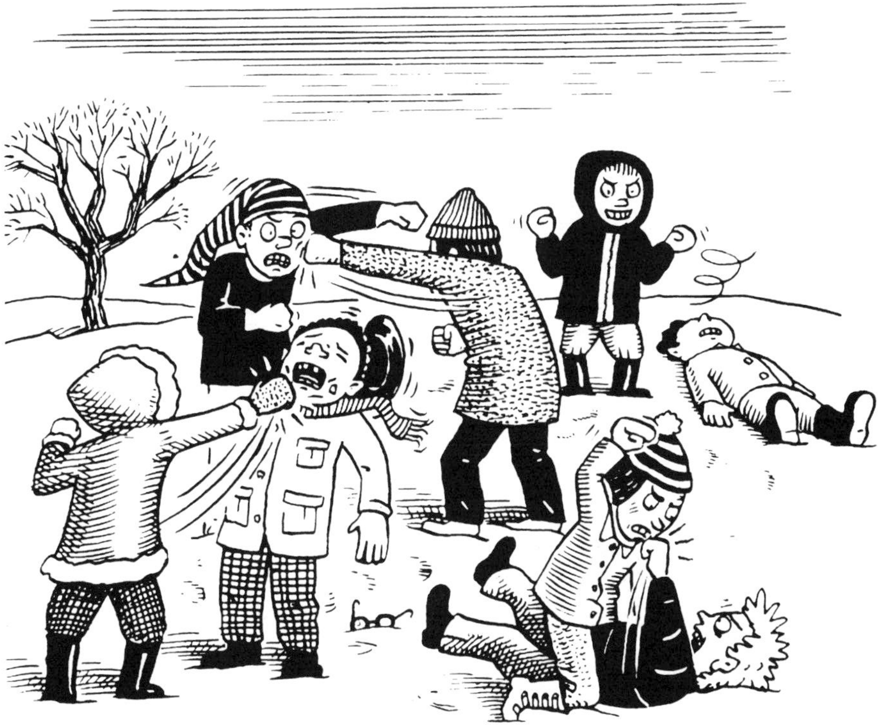

Incriminating clog marks on her back

"*Grandma Got Run Over*
By a Reindeer," ELMO & PATSY

Incriminating Claus marks on her back

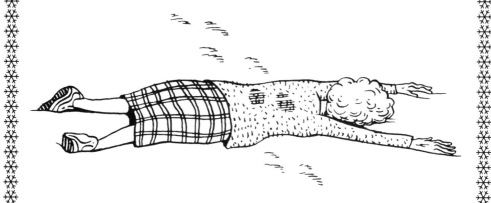

Marv is mighty bitter, perfumed

"We Three Kings"

Myrrh is mine, its bitter perfume

Tavernly host

"Silent Night"

Heavenly host

He was bored, bored, bored in Bethlehem

"Children Go Where I Send Thee"

He was born, born, born in Bethlehem

69

Feed the worms

"Do They Know It's Christmas?"

BAND AID

Feed the world

Good King Wenceslas looked out
on the feet of heathens

"Good King Wenceslas"

---

*Good King Wenceslas looked out
on the feast of Stephen*

Strike the heart, enjoy the florist

"Deck the Halls"

Strike the harp and join the chorus

Just like the wands I used to know

"*White Christmas*"

Just like the ones I used to know

You're erotic, Mr. Grinch

"You're a Mean One, Mr. Grinch"

You're a rotter, Mr. Grinch

Warming clover, if you want it

"Happy Xmas (War Is Over),"

JOHN & YOKO/THE PLASTIC ONO BAND

War is over, if you want it

✳ Oh, tanned and bound

✳ Oh, atom bomb

"*O Tannenbaum*"

O Tannenbaum

Joy to the pumps and joy to the skis

"*Oi to the World,*" NO DOUBT

Oi to the punks and oi to the skins

Got fleas on my dog,
toss spittle on you and a freezing dog

"Feliz Navidad"

Feliz Navidad, próspero año y felicidad

While shepherds washed their socks by night

"While Shepherds Watched Their Flocks"

While shepherds watched their flocks by night

Sudsy CAMEL SOAP

They sold him the baffled ham

"I Saw Three Ships"

They sailed into Bethlehem

Wonder Bread for a new and glorious mom

"O Holy Night"

Yonder breaks for a new and glorious morn

Serpents left their flocks and
came to see and worship him

"Once Upon a Christmas,"

KENNY ROGERS AND DOLLY PARTON

---

*Shepherds left their flocks and
came to see and worship him*

They'll be stalking you fine

"*Santa Claus Go Straight to the Ghetto,*" JAMES BROWN

Fill every stocking you find

Six geezers lying

"The Twelve Days of Christmas"

Six geese a-laying

Frosty the Snowman is a ferret elf, I say

"Frosty the Snowman"

Frosty the Snowman is a fairy tale, they say

Pees on earth, and then he smiles

"*Hark! The Herald Angels Sing*"

Peace on earth, and mercy mild

83

You would even say it blows

"Rudolph the Red-Nosed Reindeer"

You would even say it glows

Decorations are on my Defiant

"Christmas All Over Again,"

TOM PETTY AND THE HEARTBREAKERS

Decorations are hung by the fire

A nuder dame to see

"The Little Drummer Boy"

A newborn King to see

To go blind in a one-horse sleigh

"Jingle Bell Rock"

To go glidin' in a one-horse sleigh

Let nothing through this May

"God Rest Ye Merry, Gentlemen"

Let nothing you dismay

Onward Christmas soldiers, Margie has to wash

"Onward Christian Soldiers"

Onward Christian soldiers, marching as to war

Santa Claus is comin' to tan

"*Santa Claus Is Comin' to Town*"

Santa Claus is comin' to town

No giving things to
all the listless boys you bring

"I Just Called to Say I Love You,"

STEVIE WONDER

*No giving thanks for
all the Christmas joys you bring*

Gone away is the bluebird,
here to stay is the nude bird

"*Winter Wonderland*"

---

*Gone away is the bluebird,
here to stay is a new bird*

When a poor man came in sight,
gathering wine and gruel

"*Good King Wenceslas*"

---

*When a poor man came in sight,
gathering winter fuel*

Outside the snow is falling
and friends are calling "You fool!"

"Sleigh Ride"

---

*Outside the snow is falling
and friends are calling "Yoo-hoo"*

93

The elephants we had last year

"Christmas (Baby Please Come Home)"

All the fun we had last year

The witch his mother Mary,
he'd never take in scorn

"God Rest Ye Merry, Gentlemen"

The which his mother Mary,
did nothing take in scorn

Now the world is quilted

"Christmastime," SMASHING PUMPKINS

Now the word is given

Christ our savior is born horned

"Silent Night"

Christ our savior is born

Won't be the same beer,
if you're not here with me

"Blue Christmas"

Won't be the same here,
if you're not here with me

He's got to wear his goggles
'cause the snow really bites

"Little Saint Nick," THE BEACH BOYS

He's got to wear his goggles
'cause the snow really flies

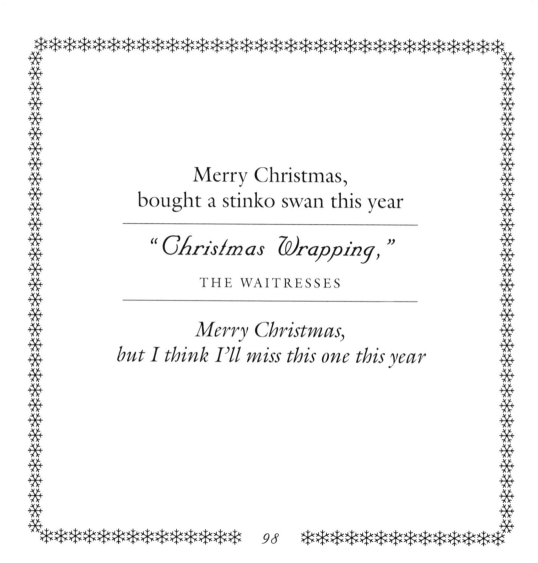

Merry Christmas,
bought a stinko swan this year

"Christmas Wrapping,"

THE WAITRESSES

Merry Christmas,
but I think I'll miss this one this year

She didn't see me creep
down the stairs to have a pee

"I Saw Mommy Kissing Santa Claus"

*She didn't see me creep
down the stairs to have a peek*

Burly hulks say "Hallelujah!"

_____

"Silent Night"

_____

Heavenly hosts sing "Hallelujah!"

How still we see the lice

_____

"O Little Town of Bethlehem"

_____

How still we see thee lie

It's Christmastime, no need to be a freak

"Do They Know It's Christmas?" BAND AID

It's Christmastime, no need to be afraid

Some bodies wait for you

"A Holly Jolly Christmas"

Somebody waits for you

Everybody knows a turkey,
handsome Mr. Soul

"The Christmas Song"

*Everybody knows,
a turkey and some mistletoe*

We wish you a very crisp mess

"*We Wish You a Merry Christmas*"

We wish you a merry Christmas

Write down: "Santa Claus laid"

"*Here Comes Santa Claus*"

Right down Santa Claus Lane

Wanda blames him: Lose the lube

"*The Chipmunk Song (Christmas Don't Be Late),*" THE CHIPMUNKS

Want a plane that loops the loop

✳ Oh, what fun it is to ride
with one horse, soap, and hay

✳ Oh, what fun it is to ride
in one whore's open sleigh

"Jingle Bells"

Oh, what fun it is to ride
in a one-horse open sleigh

Shitty sidewalks, busy sidewalks

"Silver Bells"

City sidewalks, busy sidewalks

Big fat Santa is on his way

"Santa Claus Is Comin' to Town,"

PEGGY LEE

Think that Santa is on his way

✳ Hark, the harried angels sing

✳ Hark there, Harold's angel sings

"Hark! The Herald Angels Sing"

Hark! The herald angels sing

O my twin-Christ was born

"O Holy Night"

O night when Christ was born

Walkin' in a woman's underwear

"Winter Wonderland"

Walkin' in a winter wonderland

Do you steal what I steal?

"*Do You Hear What I Hear?*"

Do you see what I see?

Your bowels so green in sunshine

"*Oh Christmas Tree*"

Your boughs so green in sunshine

✳ Got rusty, merry gentlemen

✳ God dress ye merry gentlemen

"*God Rest Ye Merry, Gentlemen*"

God rest ye merry, gentlemen

For Christ is born of Mary
and gathered in a glove

"O Little Town of Bethlehem"

---

*For Christ is born of Mary
and gathered all above*

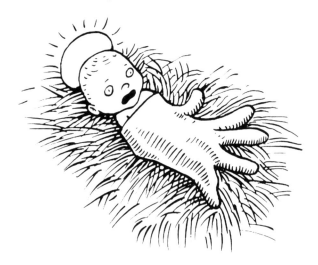

More on Mounties

"We Three Kings"

Moor and mountain

❄ Good tidings we bring to you and your kid

❄ Good tidings we bring to you and your king

"We Wish You a Merry Christmas"

Good tidings we bring to you and your kin

Better watch out for poor elves!

"Grandma Got Run Over
By a Reindeer," ELMO & PATSY

Better watch out for yourselves!

Holey and lint, sewed tender and mild

"Silent Night"

Holy infant, so tender and mild

And a cartridge in a pantry

"The Twelve Days of Christmas"

And a partridge in a pear tree

Eat the salmon toy

"Joy to the World"

Repeat the sounding joy

Bells on Bob's tail ring

"Jingle Bells"

Bells on bobtails ring

Appendix:
It's Beginning to Sound
a Lot Like Christmas

Dancing with nice elves

"*Dancing with Myself,*" BILLY IDOL

Dancing with myself

Christmas is over

"*Crimson and Clover,*" JOAN JETT

Crimson and clover

How'd you get Rudolph to wreck Kris?

"*Rudie Can't Fail,*" THE CLASH

How you get so rude and a-reckless?

I've been downhearted, babe,
every Christmas day

"*Standing Outside a Broken Phone
Booth with Money in My Hand,*"

PRIMITIVE RADIO GODS

---

*I've been downhearted, babe,
ever since the day*

She'll interview for the part of Santa

"*Secret Garden,*" BRUCE SPRINGSTEEN

She'll let you into the parts of herself

Santa Claus for adventure

Theme from "The Love Boat"

Set a course for adventure

Acknowledgments

In case you think that I have spent every Christmas season for the last ten years in a hallucinogenic haze, I must spread the credit (or perhaps, the blame) for the mishearings in *Deck the Halls with Buddy Holly*. I was not solely responsible for the mondegreens in this book; in fact, there is a substantial list of Santa's Little Helpers. I would like to thank the following people for sharing their seasonal errors:

Marcia Abbate, Judy Austin, Holly Baca, Lee-Merle Barwis, Jennifer Bourne, Don Casalone, Donald Clark, Hal Cochran, Jennifer Daniher and friends, Wick Davis, Justin Ezzi, Beth Follet and the Crumps, Melissa Freitas, Ted Friedman, Dan Grabon, Christina Hansen, Anne Hayes, J. Jasso, Babs Klein, Bruce A. Lafitte, Andrew E. Larsen, Ruth Levine, Julie Levy-Weston, Kate Lewis, Phill Mayhall, Christy McDaniel, McKenzie Milanowski, Patricia and Dottie Miller, Audrey Null, Kristen Radoccia, Susan and Adam Rose, Sheila Rosen, Diane Smith, Tina W. Stevens, Doug Welbaum, and Regina Williams.

If you have musical mishearings of your own, I would love to include them in a future volume, whether they come from love ballads, country songs, or old punk singles. Please send them to me, Gavin Edwards, at P.O. Box 023291, Brooklyn, NY 11202–3291. But don't delay—as always, I can acknowledge only the first person to send me each misheard lyric.

I would like to offer my heartfelt thanks to artist Ted Stearn, both for his delightfully demented illustrations and for being a pleasure to work with. If you enjoyed his art and would like to see more of it, I recommend his excellent "Fuzz and Pluck" comic, recently collected by Fantagraphics Books. If your local comic store doesn't have it, send a check for $13.95 to Fantagraphics at 7563 Lake City Way NE, Seattle, WA 98115—and mention this book.

I am most pleased that *Deck the Halls with Buddy Holly* marks the return of a prodigal daughter to the mondegreen fold: editor Laureen Connelly Rowland, who previously distinguished herself on *He's Got the Whole World in His Pants*. Her enthusiasm is the reason this book exists; her intelligence and keen eye improved it in a thousand ways.

My agent, Gordon Kato, is a keen businessman, a trusted advisor, and a prince among men. Furthermore, he's a jolly old soul. He denies hanging around the North Pole, but I suspect that he's secretly Kris Kringle.

This book is my first with HarperCollins; I would like to thank all the good people who work there and put so much effort into bringing this volume to print and getting it out to the bookstores, especially Susan Weinberg, Rick Pracher, Margaret Mirabile, Laura Lindgren, Jodi Anderson, and Jen Hart. I hope they all get what they hope for in their Christmas stockings.

I started this book in Brooklyn and finished it in London. I want to thank everybody on both sides of the Atlantic who made my journey not just possible but pleasant, especially Tim Armstrong, Fiona Smith, Chris Heath, Valerie Phillips, Andrew Harrison, Guida Swan, Michael Caruso, Michael Guy, Kirin Buckley, Rob Sheffield, Michael Hainey, Sara Nolan, Ilsa Enomoto, Scraps DeSelby, Steve Doberstein, Kathleen Ryan, Ted Friedman, and Kate Lewis.

And most of all, I would like to thank my wonderful girlfriend, Jill McManus. Despite her initial doubts about this book ("There's nothing to talk about except mistletoe and that jive Santa Claus shit"), it wouldn't exist without her counsel and aid. She double-checked correct lyrics and kept me sane; the words "thank you" seem slightly inadequate. So instead I say, "You make every day like Christmas."

Index